DATE DUE

DEMCO 38-296

RON MILLER

EXTRASOLAR PLANETS

WORLDS BEYOND

TWENTY-FIRST CENTURY BOOKS   BROOKFIELD, CONNECTICUT

This book is dedicated to Benjamin Miller.

Illustrations by Ron Miller. Photographs courtesy of NASA.

Library of Congress Cataloging-in-Publication Data
Miller, Ron, 1947-
Extrasolar planets / by Ron Miller.
p. cm. – (Worlds beyond)
Includes index.
Summary: Chronicles the discoveries of all the planets within our solar system, as well as
planets beyond our system.
ISBN 0-7613-2354-6 (lib. bdg.)
Extrasolar planets—Juvenile literature. [1. Planets.] I. Title.
QB820 .M55 2002
523—dc21
2001031685

Published by Twenty-First Century Books
A Division of The Millbrook Press, Inc.
2 Old New Milford Road
Brookfield, Connecticut 06804
www.millbrookpress.com

CONTENTS

CHAPTER ONE

THE DISCOVERY OF THE SOLAR SYSTEM

Thousands of years ago, before city lights drowned out the night sky and television kept people indoors, everyone looked at the **stars**. They were as familiar as the movie stars or rock stars of today, so of course people quickly noticed if anything strange or unusual occurred among them. While stars differed in brightness and color, they were all fixed motionless in the sky. The same stars always appeared in the same relationship to one another, night after night. All except for five. These strange bodies constantly changed position, but the difference was very slight because they moved so slowly. It took weeks or even months to identify their movement—but they *did* move. The Greeks named these moving stars *planetes*, which translates as wanderers.

The five **planets** were named after Greek and Roman gods. Venus, the brightest one, was named for the goddess of love and beauty. Mars, the red planet, was named for the god of war. The second brightest, Jupiter, was named for the chief of all gods, while Mercury, the planet that appeared to move most swiftly through the sky, was named for the messenger of the gods. Finally, the name Saturn came from the Roman god of agriculture.

It is difficult to define the term planets, and the more effort made to keep the definition simple, the more difficult it gets. One attempt at a simple description claims that a planet is any nonluminous body that orbits a star and is typically a small fraction of the star's **mass**. But this definition includes objects that are not usually considered planets. Asteroids and comets, for example, fit this definition, and they are certainly not what we mean by the word planet.

The most useful definition maintains that planets must be massive enough to have once had a molten core, which differentiated the interior of the planet from its exterior. This means that the heavier elements, such as iron, sank to the core while the lighter elements, such as aluminum and silicon, rose to the surface. Accordingly, all planets should have a dense rocky/metallic core. **Asteroids**, on the other hand, are chunks of rock and metal debris left over from the creation of the **solar system**—they are entirely made of rock or metal. **Comets** are not planets either; they are simply huge icebergs.

Planets formed far enough from their stars might have retained their original dense atmosphere of hydrogen and helium. This means that there are two classes of planets: **terrestrial planets**, like Earth, Venus, or Mars, lost their original atmospheres and have rocky surfaces; and **gas giants**, like Jupiter and Saturn, have small rocky or metallic cores surrounded by deep blankets of gas or liquid. Most of the large **moons** in the solar system are similar to terrestrial planets, but they orbit the Sun instead of another planet. Indeed, several moons are larger than the planets Mercury and Pluto!

Brown dwarfs are between gas giants and true stars. Like stars, they were created when a cloud of dust and gas collapsed under its own **gravity**, but the cloud was too small for a full-size star to form, and they never became massive enough to trigger nuclear **fusion**. They radiate energy, but only through the heat generated by their own gravity. Brown dwarfs are sometimes called "hot Jupiters" or "51 Pegasi" planets. Brown dwarfs range in size from several times the mass of Jupiter to about 13 times the mass of Jupiter—an object larger than that has enough gravity to initiate nuclear fusion and become a star.

Stars are large bodies of gas that radiate energy produced by nuclear fusion. This happens in their cores, where intense gravitational pressure and temperatures cause hydrogen nuclei to fuse into helium, in the process converting huge quantities of matter into energy. Stars are formed from vast clouds of hydrogen that collapse under the influence of their own gravity. As the **density** of the gas increases, the pressure increases and the core becomes hot—eventually hot enough for nuclear fusion to trigger. The energy radiated by the fusion process halts the collapse of the cloud, and a star is formed.

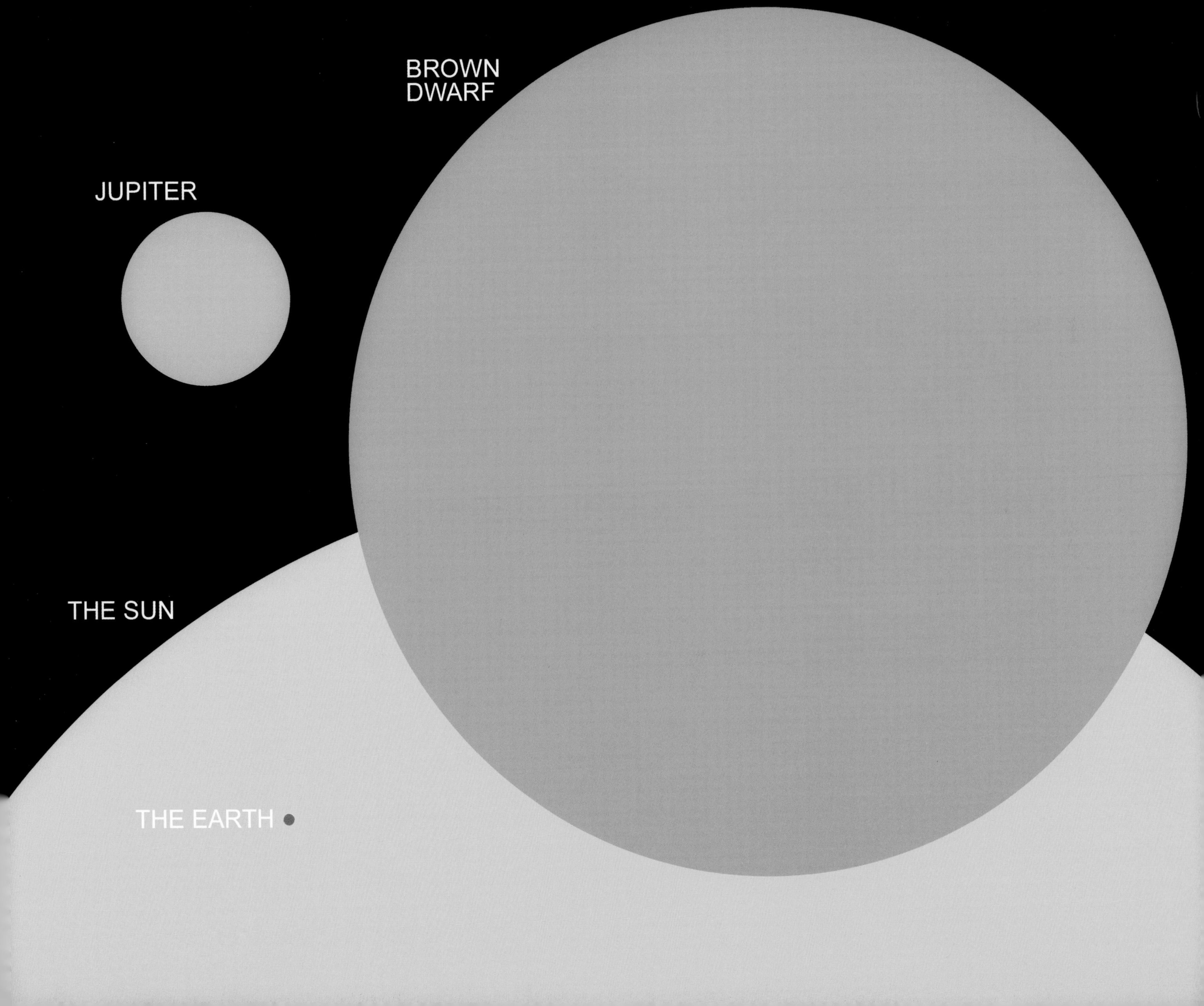
BROWN
DWARF
JUPITER
THE SUN
THE EARTH

Galileo Galilei

Because this god was at one time confused with the Greek god of time and old age, Saturn seemed an appropriate name for the planet that appeared to move the slowest though the sky.

People considered the planets interesting but of no special significance; the only thing that set them apart from the thousands of other stars was that they moved. No one ever imagined that they might in fact be other worlds. Not until the year 1610, that is.

The Italian scientist Galileo Galilei, who lived from 1564 to 1642, had been experimenting with an amazing new optical instrument recently invented in the Netherlands—the telescope. It consisted of nothing more than a pair of glass lenses set at either end of a wooden tube, but it had the remarkable property of making distant objects appear closer. The Dutch were immediately aware of its potential use to navigators and the military, but Galileo did something with the telescope that no scientist before had considered: He turned it toward the night sky. In that time, people thought the stars were nothing more than bright pinpoints of light, and everyone knew that the Moon was a polished, gleaming sphere of absolute purity (its dark markings were considered the reflection of the impure Earth). What could possibly be gained from looking at them more closely?

What Galileo learned forever changed how we regard the universe around us and even how we regard Earth. He observed that while the Moon was made of *some* pure celestial substance, it was covered with mountains and pockmarked with craters. It was, he said, "not smooth, uniform, and precisely spherical as a great number philosophers believe it (and the other heavenly bodies) to be, but is uneven, rough, and full of cavities and prominences, being not unlike the face of the earth." The planets, he found, were not just a special class of star but were in fact worlds perhaps very much like our own. They were spherical, like Earth, and some of them had vague markings that might, Galileo thought, be continents and seas. It was even more astonishing that Jupiter was not only a world, but it had moons as well—four of them (though now we know that it possesses more than a dozen)—like a miniature solar system. The moons he discovered—Ganymede, Io, Europa, and Callisto—are called the **Galilean satellites**.

The church censured Galileo's findings, but it was a time of great discoveries, so it did not take long for the information to get out. When Galileo's discoveries became widely known, people started wondering if these other worlds were like our own. Did life exist on them? Did people live there? Soon several books were published speculating about what sort of life might exist on the planets.

The great German astronomer, Johannes Kepler, wrote what may be the first science-fiction novel, *Somnium*, which was published in 1634 (a few years after his death). As a serious scientist, he described the Moon and the sort of creatures that might live there as accurately as the knowledge of the time allowed. The Moon was a very alien world, he told his readers. Nights were fifteen days long "and dreadful with uninterrupted shadow." The cold at night was more intense than anything experienced on Earth, while the heat of day was terrific. Animals that lived on the Moon adapted to these harsh conditions. Some went into hibernation, while others evolved hard shells and other protection.

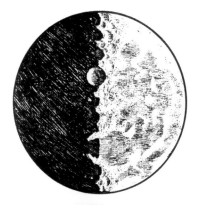

Galileo's drawings of the Moon, shown here, were the first ever made using a telescope. They showed for the first time that the Moon is a body like Earth.

Another book, written by Bernard de Fontenelle in 1686, became a best-seller. *Discourses on the Plurality of Worlds* suggested that every planet is inhabited, though not at all necessarily by life resembling that on Earth. Although he knew very little about the conditions on the planets other than their sizes and distances from the Sun, he made a lot of speculations. The people of Jupiter, he suggested, hardly ever get to know one another since the planet is so large, while, on the other hand, Mercury is so small that everyone knows everyone else. Saturn, the most distant planet from the Sun (or so it was thought at the time), was so cold that if any of its creatures were to visit Earth they would die of the heat. Because of the cold on their planet, he decided, Saturnians live and die without ever moving from the place they were born.

Books like these—both fanciful and realistic—helped convince their readers that other worlds did exist and that it was possible there might be life on them. People even began to wonder if the stars themselves might be other suns. After all, they asked, if the universe has an infinite number of stars why couldn't some of them be suns like our own? And if they are suns like ours, couldn't they also have planets circling them?

More Planets?

Astronomy's knowledge of the planets grew as telescopes improved. An astonishing discovery was made in 1781. While surveying the stars with a homemade telescope no larger than one an amateur astronomer might use today, the British astronomer William Herschel discovered an entirely new planet, one that no one had ever suspected existed. Scientists hadn't bothered to look for other planets because they assumed there *couldn't* be any others. The five known planets along with the Sun and Earth equaled seven bodies altogether, a mystical number that seemed perfect to many people.

At first Herschel thought he had discovered a new comet, but when he worked out its orbit he realized that it had to be a planet. Comets have highly elliptical orbits that are very different from the nearly circular orbits of most planets. Herschel's news took the world by storm and there was a rush to name the new planet. Georgium, for King George III, and Herschel, for the astronomer, were two popular candidates, but finally it was named Uranus, for the Greek god of the sky—much to William's relief.

William Herschel

Uranus can barely be detected by the naked eye, and is so faint and so distant that its motion among the stars is hardly noticeable. Yet, old records showed that Uranus had been observed many times in the past, for at least a century, but had not been recognized for what it was. When the records were reviewed more carefully, something strange was revealed: Uranus didn't seem to move along with the orbit predicted by the calculations. It wasn't exactly in the position, in 1781 and years following, that the numbers anticipated. In some years it seemed to lag behind, and in other years it seemed to move too quickly. Where was the mistake being made and how? In 1834 the Reverend T. J. Hussey of Kent, England, made a startling suggestion: The fault wasn't in the mathematics at all. What if there was yet one more unknown planet orbiting beyond Uranus? Its gravitational pull upon Uranus might account for the inaccuracies.

John Couch Adams

Urbain Le Verrier

Hussey suggested that it might be possible to predict the location of this mysterious planet by working backward from its effect on Uranus. A brilliant young math student at Cambridge University, John Couch Adams, took up the challenge and by 1843 had worked out precisely where he thought the new planet ought to be. He sent his results to George Airy, the British Astronomer Royal (the official astronomer of the royal court). Airy did nothing with Adams's calculations until 1846, when the French astronomer, Urbain Le Verrier, published the results of his own calculations. Le Verrier used the same reasoning that Adams had, and the location he predicted for the new planet was almost exactly the same. As soon as Airy learned of this, he assigned two astronomers—James Challis and William Lassell—to search for the unidentified planet.

Challis recorded an observation of the new planet on August 4 and again on August 12, but failed to check his observations. In the meantime, however, Johann Galle and Heinrich d'Arrest, of the Berlin Observatory in Germany, using Le Verrier's figures, found and identified the planet. Then the problems began.

Adams had been the first to predict the location of the new planet, while it was Le Verrier's work that actually led to its discovery. A major international dispute broke out (neither Adams nor Le Verrier took part) as to whether France or England should claim credit for the new finding. Germany also put in a bid, since a pair of German astronomers actually found the planet. The French wanted to name it Le Verrier, but other countries protested. Tradition and good sense won out, and the planet was named Neptune, after the Roman god of the sea.

The discovery of Neptune was a triumph for mathematics and scientific reasoning. Astronomers became confident that what had been done once might be done again. "There is no reason," Le Verrier wrote shortly after his discovery, "to believe that this planet is the last one in the solar system. This success allows us to hope that after thirty or forty years of observation of the new planet, we should be able to use it in its turn for discovering the planet next in order of distance from the sun."

In fact, it took 82 years.

A False Start

Fame was showered on Neptune's discoverers, and many astronomers became eager to find other new planets. Instead of looking farther from the Sun, beyond Neptune, many astronomers looked closer for a planet orbiting the Sun nearer than Mercury. It had long been observed that there were unexplained disturbances to Mercury's orbit. These were similar to the disturbances of Uranus's orbit that led to the discovery of Neptune. Many assumed that an unknown planet was causing the disturbances.

The problem with trying to observe a planet close to the Sun is caused by the Sun itself—its glare makes it almost impossible to see anything near it. Mercury is difficult to observe, and anything closer to the Sun is even more so. One possibility existed: Every now and then, the orbits of Mercury and Venus cause them to pass in front of the Sun as seen from Earth. When this happens, the planets appear like tiny round black dots against the bright face of the Sun. Using telescopes especially equipped to observe the Sun,

Johann Galle

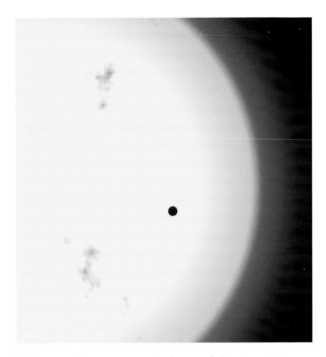
When a planet passes in front of the Sun, it is visible from Earth as a small black dot.

astronomers started searching the face of the Sun, looking for an unfamiliar small black dot.

Astronomers searched for nearly half a century without finding anything. In 1859 startling news came from an amateur astronomer in France. Edmund Lescarbault announced that he had discovered the new planet. He claimed that he saw a small round black spot cross the face of the Sun at a time when neither Mercury nor Venus would have been visible. He convinced several leading astronomers that his observation was correct, including Urbain Le Verrier, who proposed naming it Vulcan, after the Roman god of fire. Le Verrier identified what he believed were earlier observations of Vulcan, and from these he calculated its orbit. He predicted that it would reappear on March 29, April 2, and April 7, 1860. Hundreds of astronomers scrutinized the Sun on those dates, but Vulcan failed to appear. In fact, no one ever saw it again.

What then did Lescarbault see? It's hard to say now, almost a century and a half later, but it is likely that he mistook a small sunspot for a new planet.

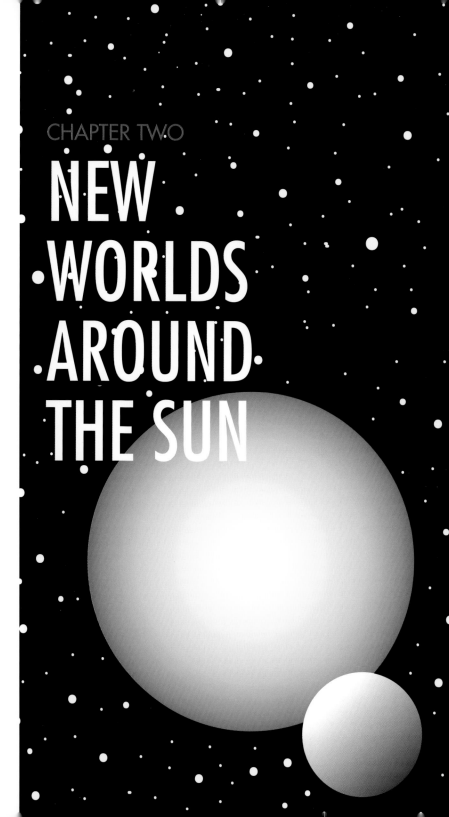

CHAPTER TWO

NEW WORLDS AROUND THE SUN

The search for a planet beyond Neptune was considered hopeless for quite a while. The planets that are farthest from their star move much slower in their orbits, so it would take a very long time for Neptune to move enough in its orbit for astronomers to be able to detect any disturbances. Mercury, the planet closest to the Sun, orbits it in a mere 88 days. Earth, almost three times farther away, takes 365 days, while Neptune takes 165 *years*, twice as long as Uranus. Yet in the early twentieth century a wealthy amateur astronomer from Boston took up the challenge to find a planet beyond Neptune.

Percival Lowell, a brilliant mathematician, graduated from Harvard in 1876 with honors, and then managed his family's cotton mills and electric companies. Finding this boring, he returned to a prior interest in astronomy and decided to make it his career. He specialized in the planet Mars. With his wealth, he built and funded his own observatory near Flagstaff, Arizona, on a 7,000-foot (2,134-meter) elevation he called "Mars Hill." (The observatory continues in operation to this day.) From there he carefully observed the red planet. He discovered that a network of "canals"

Percival Lowell at the telescope in Lowell Observatory, which he built to observe the planet Mars

crisscrossed Mars, and determined that they must have been constructed by intelligent beings. This shook the world's imagination . . . but that's another story.

Lowell began to wonder if it was possible to determine the existence of a new outer planet by ignoring Neptune and focusing on Uranus. He would have to calculate the planet's orbit with a great deal more accuracy than either Adams or Le Verrier did. Any disturbances in Uranus, however slight, that Neptune could not account for must be caused by yet another planet, he reasoned. His calculations took him years, but in 1905 Lowell announced that he had determined the orbit of Planet X. What was more, he even proposed to give an exact description of the planet. It was, he said, a small world 4 billion miles (6.4 billion kilometers) from the Sun—more than 40 times farther than Earth—taking 282 years to make a single orbit. Something so small and so far away would be extremely faint.

But Lowell had a significant advantage over his predecessors. Adams and Le Verrier had to do their observations manually, meticulously marking on star charts the location of the dim object they were observing. No matter how carefully they did this or how accurate their charts were, it was an extraordinarily difficult and laborious task and always subject to inaccuracies—the observations were only as good as their eyes and their charts. But Percival Lowell had cameras. He just had to take a picture each night of a specific part of the sky. By carefully comparing photographs, he could tell if any of the tens of thousands of points of light had moved.

It was still a daunting task. Even on a photographic plate, the object for which Lowell searched was small and dim. And, as it turned out, it wasn't as easy as he had confidently expected. Failing to find his new planet by 1908, Lowell reviewed his calculations, which this time included unaccountable changes in Neptune's orbit. But he still had not found the planet, and by the time he died in 1916, Planet X remained undiscovered.

Other astronomers tried to pick up where Lowell had left off but they met no better success. Interest in the new planet slowly died out. Excitement rekindled in 1929, when a new telescope was installed at Lowell Observatory—which was running on a trust fund set up by its founder. The 13-inch (33-cm) lens camera telescope could detect objects many times dimmer than the instrument Lowell used. A 23-year-old astronomer named Clyde Tombaugh was appointed to resume the search for Planet X.

Even with modern equipment, Tombaugh's duty was Herculean. The camera photographed a small portion of the night sky. Two or three days later, exactly the same location would be photographed again. Tombaugh would place the two photographs into a device called a **blink comparator**. He compared them by flipping the images back and forth quickly, like the frames in an animated cartoon. Fixed points of light, such as stars, appeared unchanged. But if something had moved between the two exposures it appeared to "jump" back and forth as the photographic plates were compared. The process is not as easy as it sounds. Each image contained as many as 160,000 tiny points of light—or 400,000 if any part of the Milky Way was in the

The young Clyde Tombaugh around the time he discovered Pluto

plate. All of which had to be carefully examined, since any motion was extremely small and difficult to detect. The project took an entire year.

On February 18, 1930, Tombaugh was examining a pair of plates taken of a region in the constellation Gemini when he saw a tiny speck of light jump as he compared the images. It was a miniscule difference, scarcely 0.14 inch (0.36 cm). He compared the plate with others taken of the same area to make certain that he wasn't being fooled by a flaw in the photographic emulsion. The same faint spot appeared in all the plates. Tombaugh's observation was confirmed, and on March 13, 1930—the anniversary of Lowell's death—Lowell Observatory announced that Planet X had been discovered. It was named Pluto, after the god of the underworld (and, not coincidentally, because its first two letters were Percival Lowell's initials).

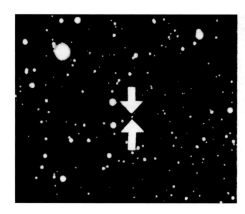

The Pluto discovery plate: The arrows show the movement of the tiny speck of light that revealed the existence of the new planet to Clyde Tombaugh.

Beyond Pluto?

Are there any planets beyond Pluto? At the time that Clyde Tombaugh discovered Pluto, most astronomers thought that even if there were, it would be almost impossible to find them. It had been extremely difficult to find Pluto. Tombaugh himself flatly declared that there is no tenth planet in our solar system. But many astronomers began to wonder.

At first, it was thought that Pluto was a world about the same size as Earth—that is, with a diameter of about 8,000 miles (12,874 km). Twenty years after its discovery, this estimate was reduced to 4,000 miles (6,437 km). Now we know that Pluto is very small: only 1,400 miles (2,253 km) in diameter. It is not only the smallest of the planets, it's smaller than five of the largest moons in our solar system.

This raised a new question. Pluto is too small to have the mass required to cause the disturbances observed in the orbits of Uranus and Neptune. But if it was not Pluto, then what caused these disturbances? Several astronomers concluded that although Tombaugh had found a new planet, he hadn't found the one that Lowell believed existed. It was possible that Planet X had not yet been discovered.

Several searches were undertaken in the late 1970s and early 1980s. Most of the new planet hunters used the same blink technique that Tombaugh had, but they had much more powerful and sophisticated camera telescopes. Although no one has yet succeeded, there is still hope that Planet X will be discovered. Why hasn't it? There are several possibilities.

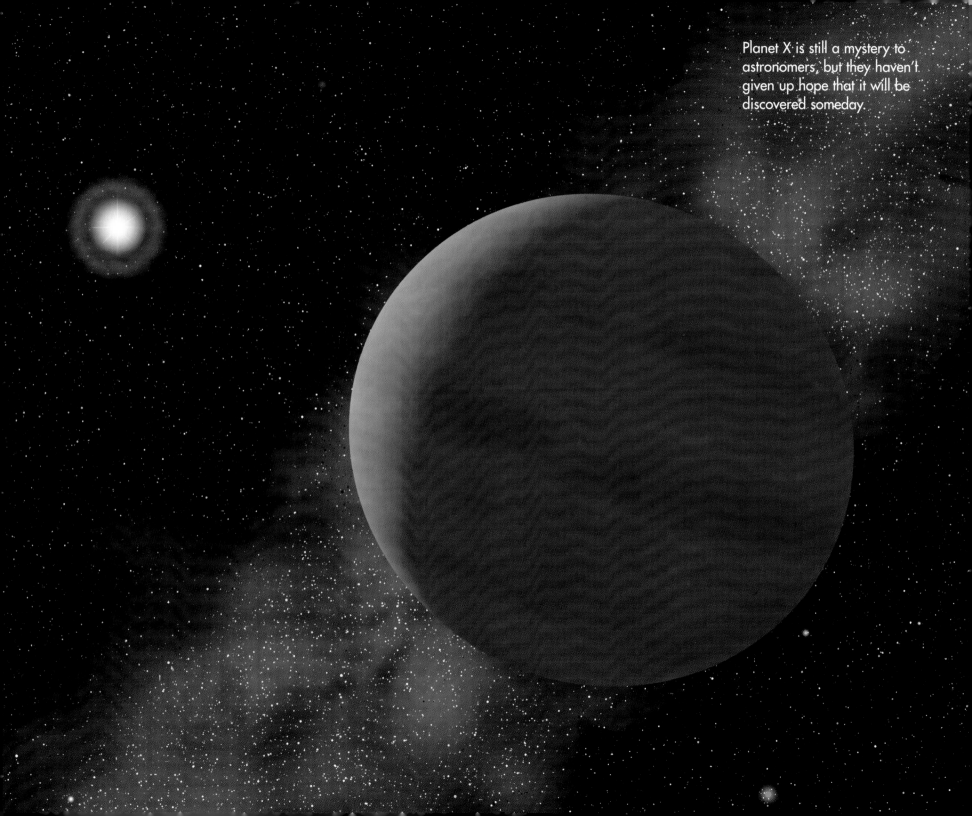

Planet X is still a mystery to astronomers, but they haven't given up hope that it will be discovered someday.

Astronomers typically work with huge distances. In fact, that's why we've come to refer to really large numbers as "astronomical." It is inconvenient to speak so often of billions or trillions of miles or kilometers, so they have devised units of measurement that are easier to handle. The one that most people are familiar with is the "light-year." This is not a measurement of time, as some believe, but the distance that light will travel in one year. Since light moves at a speed of approximately 186,000 miles (299,000 km) a *second*, this is, as you might imagine, a very large distance—about 26.5 trillion miles. Being able to say that the distance of the nearest star to Earth is 4.5 light-years is much simpler than saying that it is 119,250,000,000,000, or one hundred and nineteen trillion two hundred and fifty billion, miles.

Light-years are useful units to express distances between stars, but within solar systems their use is less convenient. For that purpose, the light-year is too big, though miles are still too small. If the speed of light served as the basis for solar-system measurement, it would be expressed in "light *hours*" or "light *minutes*." (One might say, for example, that Earth is 8 light-minutes from the Sun.) Instead, astronomers use the **astronomical unit** (or **AU**) when working on the scale of a solar system. That's the distance from Earth to the Sun— about 93 million miles (150 million km). Instead of saying that Mars is 141,500,000 miles (227,715,000 km) from the Sun, it's much simpler to say that it is 1.52 astronomical units (or AU). Mercury, which is closer to the Sun than Earth is, is 0.39AU, and Pluto, which is 3,666,000,000 miles (5,900,000,000 km) from the Sun, is at 40AU.

AUs help to visualize the size of different solar systems. Using them, we can visualize how another planet might be compared to Earth. If a planet orbits a sunlike star at 0.33AU, or one-third the distance of Earth from the Sun, you know immediately that its sun would appear to be three times larger in its sky than our Sun does in Earth's sky. A planet orbiting at 4AU would have a sun that appeared to be four times smaller than ours.

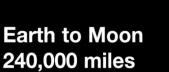

Earth to Moon
240,000 miles
384,000 km
1.3 light seconds

Earth to the Sun
93,000,000 miles
150,000,000 km
1 AU
8 light minutes

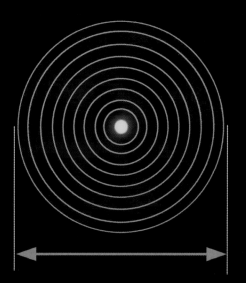

Diameter of the Solar System
7,460,000,000 miles
112,000,000,000 km
8 AU
11 light hours

Solar System to the Nearest Star
26,500,000,000,000 miles
42,600,000,000,000 km
290,000 AU
4.5 light years

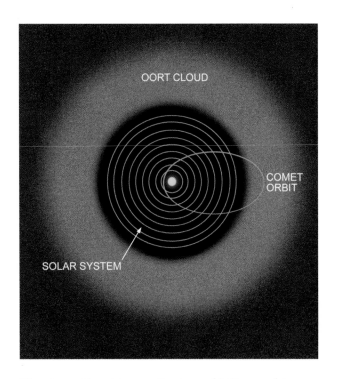

The Oort Cloud is a collection of billions of icy objects that orbit far beyond Pluto. On occasion, one will fall into the inner solar system and become a comet.

One reason Planet X hasn't been discovered yet is that its orbit is tilted so much to the plane of the solar system that the planet may lie far above or below the region where most other planets are found—an immense area to search if you don't know where to begin. Or it may be that the planet is so small and dark that it is lost when seen against the millions of stars in the Milky Way. Its orbit might be so long—perhaps a thousand years or more—that centuries would pass before it moved into a clear portion of the night sky. Finally, it might not be there at all. This is possible since spacecraft flybys of Uranus and Neptune have not yet shown disturbances to their orbits. But some astronomers still wonder. . . .

The possibility of a planet beyond Pluto involves a mystery concerning comets. The solar system is surrounded by a swarm of comets called the **Oort Cloud**, named for Jan Oort, the Dutch astronomer who discovered it in the 1950s. The cloud averages 50,000AU from Earth, which is more than a thousand times Pluto's distance from the Sun. This far from the warmth of the Sun, the comets are frozen mountains of ice and dust, like dirty icebergs. They are much too far from the Sun for its warmth to turn this ice into the gas that forms the glowing tails we usually associate with comets. Most of the comets that enter the inner solar system, such as Halley's comet, Shoemaker-Levy, or Hyukatake, originate in the Oort Cloud. What starts them on their inward spiral toward the Sun? Is there something out there disturbing the comets' routine orbits? The fact that comets have fallen out of the Oort Cloud and continue to do so may indicate the presence of an unknown planet.

(24)

Astronomer Richard Muller thinks that Planet X might be a **red dwarf** star that he has named Nemesis. It is a dim companion to the Sun, orbiting at a distance of 3 light-years. Daniel Whitmire, of the University of Louisiana, thinks that Planet X might be either a brown dwarf or a giant planet the size of Jupiter. What might this planet be like if it is really there? Whitmire suggests that if Planet X is not a brown dwarf or gas giant, it might still be a large world, perhaps five times larger than Earth, orbiting 10 billion miles (16 billion km) from the Sun (more than 100AU). Scientists such as Tom Van Flandern and Conley Powell agree that Planet X would be two to five times as massive as Earth. But they also believe that it orbits 5.5 billion miles (8.9 km) from the Sun—60 times farther away than Earth, one and a half times as far from the Sun as Pluto. It would be a dark, frigid world—so cold that oxygen would be a solid as hard as steel—where the Sun would be only a brilliant, heatless star in its sky. If it exists, Powell would like to name it after Persephone, the wife of Pluto.

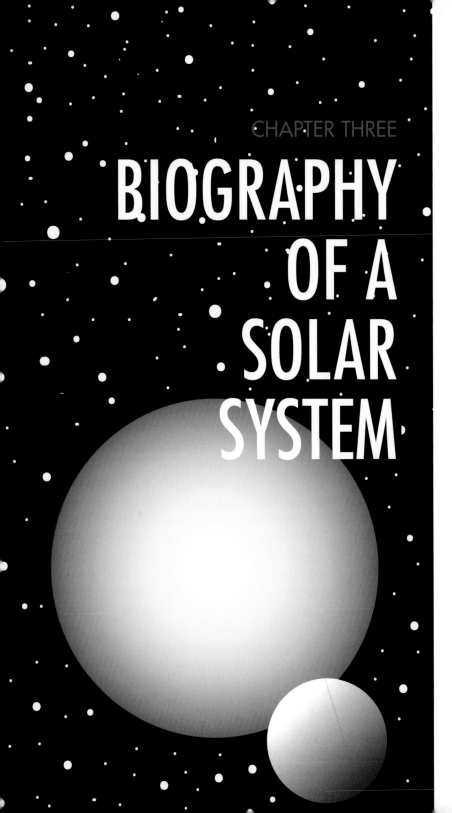

CHAPTER THREE

BIOGRAPHY OF A SOLAR SYSTEM

More than 300 years ago, philosophers and scientists suggested that the existence of our solar system implied that there might be other ones. Nowadays, it is almost impossible to imagine that our system of planets is unique. The real question is: How many other solar systems might there be? The answer depends a great deal on the knowledge of how solar systems are formed. If, for example, they are formed when two stars pass each other so closely that matter is pulled out of one by the gravitational pull of the other, then solar systems may be extremely rare.

Many theories about the origin of the solar system have been developed since it was first recognized that there *is* a solar system. One of the earliest scientific theories was proposed in 1745 by the French naturalist Georges-Louis Leclerc de Buffon, who suggested that a giant comet had once collided with the Sun, and that masses of material blown off the Sun eventually became the planets.

In 1755 Immanuel Kant developed the idea that the Sun and planets formed from a vast, nebulous cloud of dust and gas billions of miles in diameter, a theory that was further developed by Pierre Simon Laplace in 1796. As the cloud contracted under its

(26)

A nebula is an immense cloud of dust or gas that may be luminous or dark depending on whether it absorbs or reflects radiation. Nebulae can form dense knots possibly from the shock wave of a supernova. If these knots become large enough they may eventually birth a star.

own gravity, the Sun formed at the center. Meanwhile, the cloud began to rotate, which caused it to flatten out into a ring or series of rings. The planets formed within these rings and their moons formed around them the same way the planets had formed around the Sun.

The theories of Kant and Laplace held sway until the end of the nineteenth century, when they were severely criticized on mathematical grounds. In 1895 Thomas C. Chamberlin, a geologist, and Forest G. Moulton, an astronomer, together devised a radically new theory to circumvent the objections. They suggested that the solar system was the result of a near-collision of the Sun with a massive star, whose tremendous gravitation ripped a huge jet of gas from the Sun. In the wake of the wrecked Sun, the rogue star left a spiral swarm of particles that eventually coalesced into the planets we know today. The two scientists acknowledged that their theory made the creation of solar systems a rare event. "A given sun," they wrote, "will pass near enough to another sun to cause serious disturbances once in about a billion years."

This theory was widely accepted for nearly twenty years—possibly as much for its dramatic qualities as for its scientific value—but objections were soon established. In 1916 the tidal theory of Sir James Jeans and Harold Jeffreys, really just a modification of the earlier idea, gained support. The tidal theory, like all those before it, was not conclusive, but also like all previous theories, it contributed to the present view of how all solar systems, including our own, were formed.

The currently accepted theory of the evolution of the solar system takes into account most of the objections to earlier ones. It

As the knot of nebular dust and gas collapses, a rotating protoplanetary disk forms. It becomes hotter as the center grows denser. Soon it will be hot enough to trigger hydrogen fusion and a star will be born.

explains that the Sun and planets formed about 4.5 billion years ago from an enormous cloud of dust and gas. This is possible if the cloud was large enough for the gravitation of its individual particles to start the cloud contracting and then maintain the contraction. Once this process began, the cloud shrank to a millionth of its original size very quickly. During this collapse it became a **protostar**.

As the center of the cloud became denser, its gravity increased. This in turn caused it to collapse even further. Soon the core began to heat up, glowing dully red within the dark cloud. Then a nuclear reaction began—perhaps only a few thousand years after

A protoplanetary disk in the Orion Nebula as photographed by the Hubble Space Telescope: In the right image the disk was photographed through filters that allow us to see glowing nebulosities above and below. This reveals the existence of the central star, which is normally hidden from us by the dark dust. (NASA)

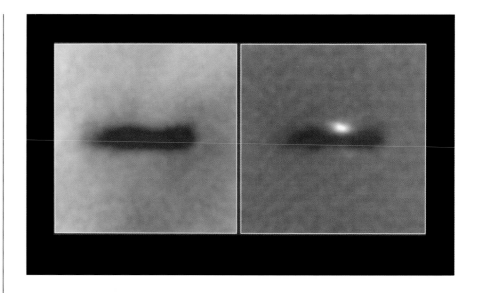

the cloud first began to condense—and when this happened, the protostar became a star. The increased amount of heat this produced created an outward pressure that resisted the collapsing dust and gas, and the collapse came to a halt. (The Hubble Space Telescope has observed other young solar systems in just this phase of development. Called **protoplanetary disks**, they are dark and bun-shaped, often with a dimly glowing center as shown above.)

Within the cloud, tiny particles of dust collided and stuck together, forming little clumps of material. As these clumps, called **planetesimals**, grew in size, they attracted more particles. This process is called **accretion**. Most of the early collisions were relatively gentle, so the planetesimals didn't become fragmented.

Dust particles in the solar
nebula settle into a disk shape
as they collide and combine
into ever larger bodies through-
out the accretion process.

Soon, enough grains of dust grew to the size of rocks, then boulders, and then asteroids miles across. The whole process of growth from the size of a large pinhead to the size of a mountain may have taken only 100,000 years or so. At this point the process began to slow down—the original dust and gas were used up and the cloud grew thin. (Several stars have been observed with large, thin disks of dust surrounding them, such as Beta Pictoris. They may be solar systems in this stage of development.)

As the planetesimals grew larger they began to move faster, and the collisions between them became more violent. Now, instead of accreting, some of them shattered into pieces. The increasing size of the planetesimals and their increasing gravity caused the higher speeds. The few planetesimals large enough to survive the collisions grew even larger, devouring the debris from the smaller objects. Once the process of accretion began, it grew very quickly. Earth may have changed from a cloud of dust to a body nearly its present size in as few as 40 million years.

Debris from the formation of the dust disk has collided to form larger and larger bodies. These eventually grow so large that their gravity shapes them into spheres. Some grow to be no larger than an asteroid or small moon, but others become as large as Earth or Jupiter.

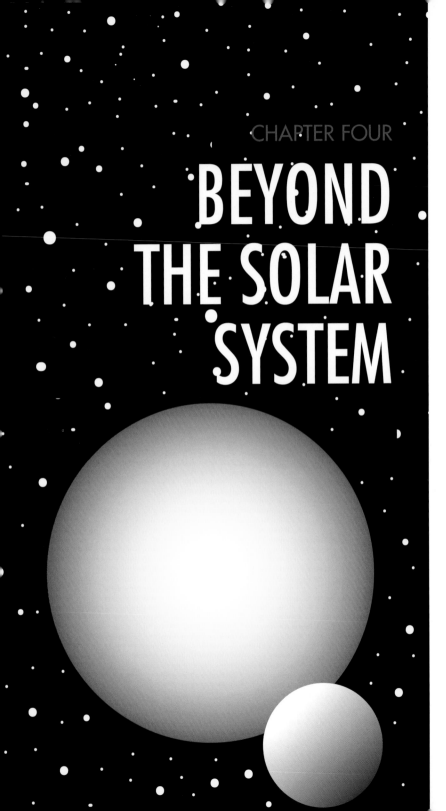

CHAPTER FOUR

BEYOND THE SOLAR SYSTEM

If solar systems do in fact form by collapse of clouds and collision of planetesimals—and all evidence seems to support this theory—they may be far more common in the universe than if Chamberlin and Moulton's theory is true. But are there, actually, planets around other stars? Until modern times, astronomers assumed that this would always be impossible to determine. Planets are dark objects that give off no light of their own and, compared to stars, are remarkably small—two factors that make planets extremely difficult to detect from Earth. Yet it *is* possible to discover objects too small and dim to be seen with even the most powerful telescope.

Sirius is the brightest star in the night sky. It is the Dog Star that accompanies the constellation Orion in winter. Like most stars—even those that appear to be completely motionless—Sirius is moving. Its motion is minimal as seen from Earth. In the course of a year, Sirius moves only about one-thirtieth of the width of a full moon. (You can visualize how small this is if you consider that a full moon appears to be about the same width as a dime held at arm's length, and in a year, Sirius appears to move only one-thirtieth of that width.)

(34)

In 1834 F. W. Bessel, a German astronomer, discovered that Sirius does not move in a uniform direction but in a somewhat wavy line. He found that the star orbits a point somewhere outside its center, which meant that it must have a companion star invisible from Earth. The two stars orbit a common center of gravity, taking about 50 years to make one orbit. You can visualize this idea by imagining a pair of balls connected by a string. If you were to throw them into the air, they would spin around one another. If one ball were painted black and one white, and you threw them into the night sky, you might not be able to see the dark ball, but you would still be able to tell it was there because of how the white ball moved.

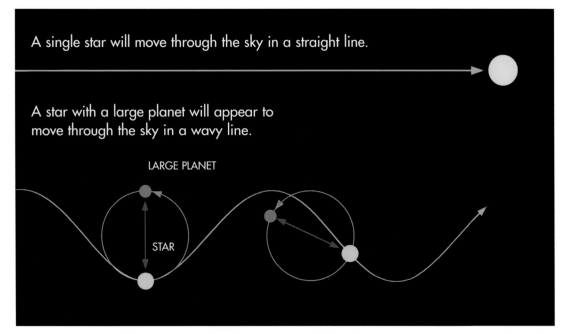

A single star will move through the sky in a straight line.

A star with a large planet will appear to move through the sky in a wavy line.

LARGE PLANET

STAR

(35)

As a planet orbits its star, the star itself appears to move from side to side. Measuring this movement is one way of detecting the presence of a planet.

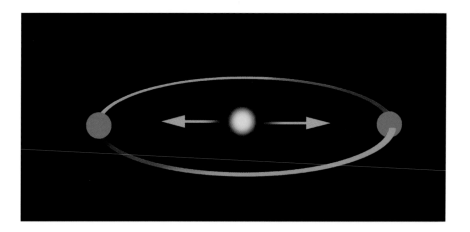

When Bessel discovered Sirius's companion star, he used a method almost identical to that by which Neptune and Pluto were found. Since the invisible object could not be observed directly, he observed its effect on Sirius and deduced its existence from that. Still, Sirius's invisible companion is not a planet. It is a **white dwarf** star, much smaller than an average star but much denser than a planet. Instruments weren't sensitive enough to detect the very tiny disturbances to a star's movement that something as small as a planet would cause until late in the twentieth century. The modern technique of measuring a star's motion is called **astrometry**.

Near the end of the twentieth century astronomical instruments became sensitive enough to detect objects with masses 100 or 200 times that of Jupiter, which is the largest planet in our solar system. (These are so large that they are probably the dim type of star called a brown dwarf rather than a true planet.) Finding an object the size of Jupiter or smaller was a more difficult task. Peter van de Kamp, an astronomer, thought he had detected one or more objects about half the mass of Jupiter orbiting Barnard's Star—the star third closest to the Sun—in the 1970s, but other astronomers have failed to confirm this.

A star can also reveal the existence of an otherwise invisible companion if the orbit of the companion passes in front of the star. When this happens, the star dims slightly. These are called **eclipsing binaries**; the star Algol is a famous example. When Algol's companion passes in front of it, the light from Algol is dimmed by one-third. But, once again, planets are far too small to cut off much of the light from their sun when they pass in front of it.

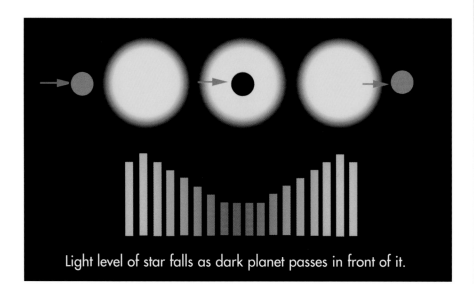

Light level of star falls as dark planet passes in front of it.

When a darker body, such as a large planet, moves between its star and Earth, the star appears to dim slightly. This dimming indicates the presence of a planet.

A third technique for detecting objects in the sky uses modern technology. Planets give off more infrared radiation than stars give off. If astronomers use a telescope sensitive to infrared radiation but insensitive to visible light, they might be able to detect the presence of a planet so near to its star that it otherwise would have been lost in the glare.

The fourth way in which astronomers can detect planets around other stars applies a phenomenon called the **Doppler effect**. The Doppler effect is the change in pitch that you hear in the sound of a train whistle or police siren as the vehicle speeds past you. As it approaches, its sound seems higher-pitched than when it's going away. This is because the wavelength of the sound is compressed as the vehicle comes toward you and stretched as it moves away. In the same way, the wavelength of light is changed by the motion of the object emitting the light. When a star is approaching you, its wavelength is shortened slightly, making the light seem a little bluer (because blue light has a shorter wavelength). When the star is moving away, the wavelength of the light is increased, making the light seem a little redder (because red light has a longer wavelength). You can't see these changes with the naked eye, but astronomers can easily detect them with an instrument called a **spectrograph**, with which they can measure the speed that distant objects are moving toward or away from us.

A star with a planet orbiting it "wobbles" a little. The motion that brings the star toward us and takes it away from us can be detected by spectrographs. Unlike the side-to-side movement of the star's wobble, which must be measured from photographs of the star—a very difficult process if the movement appears

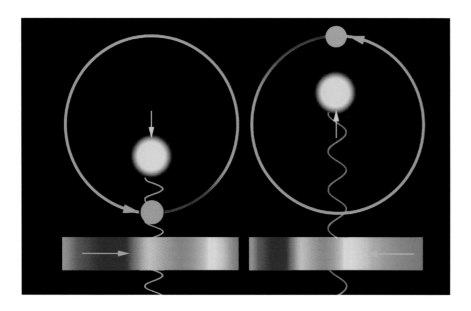

Stars move in small circles as planets orbit them. As a star moves toward Earth, its light is compressed into a shorter wavelength and looks bluer; as it moves away from Earth its light is stretched into a longer wavelength and looks redder. This Doppler shift in a star's spectrum is used to detect the presence of planets.

extremely small—the star's back-and-forth movement can be detected at any distance, as long as the star is bright enough to get a good reading. The measurement of Doppler shift changes has been the method most used in the modern search for **extrasolar** planets.

Are we alone in the universe? Is ours the only solar system? Is Earth the only planet with life? At the end of the twentieth century, it appeared that astronomers were about to provide an answer. It's a simple question with profound possibilities. As the famous science fiction author, Arthur C. Clarke, observed, "Sometimes I think we're alone in the universe, and sometimes I think we're not. In either case the idea is quite staggering."

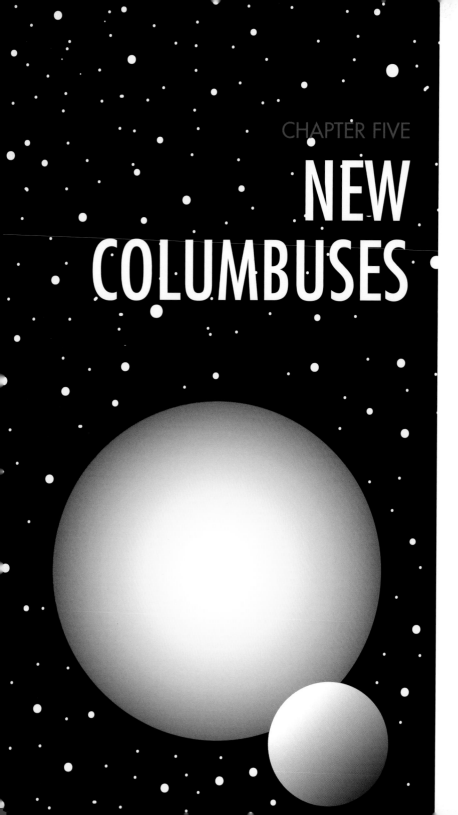

CHAPTER FIVE

NEW COLUMBUSES

Evidence and logic both indicated that there *should* be planets around other stars. Still, there had never been an unambiguous observation of one, and at the end of the 1980s, astronomers were still searching. In 1983 it was discovered that the star Beta Pictoris had a thin disk of dust surrounding it. Scientists considered such a disk the by-product of planetary formation, so it seemed likely that Beta Pictoris might have planets orbiting it. But if it did, they were undetectable. Their existence might just be wishful thinking.

Using Doppler shift measurements, it was shown that some stars have at least one object orbiting them, but in most cases these objects are very large—many times the size of Jupiter (the largest planet in our solar system, Jupiter is 318 times the mass of Earth). It has to follow that these are not true planets but instead are brown dwarfs—objects much bigger than planets but not quite large enough for their gravity to ignite the nuclear fires and form stars. Like planets, they formed from collapsing clouds of dust. Also like planets, they do not give off any heat or light from the fusion of hydrogen atoms. Instead, they are heated by **gravitational contraction**. Because they are, in effect, failed stars, brown dwarfs are also called "sub-stellar objects." Although the planet

(40)

Beta Pictoris has a thin disk of dust
surrounding it that might contain planets.

Most newly discovered extrasolar planets are compared with Jupiter. The comparison is not, however, in *size* but in *mass*. Mass measures how much material an object contains. All objects, including human beings, have mass. Floating in space, mass has no weight. But in the gravity field of another mass, such as that of a planet, mass acquires weight. This is really the measurement of how much one mass is pulling another one toward it. The weight you read on a bathroom scale is a measurement of how much Earth is pulling your mass toward it. (You are pulling against Earth, too, but it outmasses you by several billion times so it's also outpulling you by several billion times.) Jupiter is nearly 318 times as massive as Earth, while Earth's mass equals that of Venus, Mars, Mercury, and the Moon combined.

Mass is related to density. Density indicates how tightly packed the material in an object is. Two balls may be of equal size, but if one is made of lead and the other of wood, the lead ball will weigh more, because it is more massive. For the wood ball to weigh as much as the lead ball—or, in other words, to be equally massive—it would have to be a great deal larger than the lead one. A 1-pound rock and a 1-pound feather pillow have equal masses (we know that because Earth is pulling on them equally), but since the material that makes up the rock is packed much more densely than the feathers that make up the pillow, the rock is much smaller.

Likewise, two planets may be equally massive, but if one is made mostly of gas (like Jupiter) and the other mostly of rock and iron (like Earth), the first one must be much larger than the second. When an extrasolar planet is said to be "two times Jupiter's mass," it doesn't necessarily mean that the planet is twice as big as Jupiter. It means that if the two planets could be put on a scale, the planet would weigh twice as much as Jupiter. The average density of the inner planets of our solar system, including Earth, lies between that of iron and water, but Saturn's average density is less than that of water. If you could find an ocean big enough to hold it, Saturn would float!

Gravity, as we've seen, is created by the mass of a planet. The more mass it has, the greater its pull of gravity is. The Moon is only one-sixth as massive as Earth, so if you weigh 100 pounds (45.4 kg) on Earth, you would weigh only 17 pounds (7.7 kg) on the Moon. On the other hand, you would weigh 254 pounds (115 kg) on Jupiter. You may immediately spot a discrepancy here: If Jupiter is 318 times as massive as Earth, why does your weight increase by only 2.5 times instead of more than 300? The reason has to do with Jupiter's density. The force of gravity falls off rapidly with distance—the farther you are away from a mass, the less it pulls on you. If you move twice as far away from a planet, for instance, its force of gravity is one-fourth (2^2); it's the square of the distance. If you move twice that again, or four times farther away, gravity is reduced to one-sixteenth (4^2). Since Jupiter is made mostly of gas, its surface—which is really the top of a thick layer of clouds—is many thousands of miles from its massive core.

hunters did not find planets, the search showed that they were on the right track and that their techniques worked.

In 1990, at the Arecibo Radio Telescope in Puerto Rico, the astronomer Alex Wolszczan made an astonishing discovery while studying **pulsars**. Pulsars are strange objects—tiny, fast-spinning stars that emit a powerful beam of radio energy as they rotate. Their beam sweeps the sky like the beam of light from a lighthouse. Just as the light from a lighthouse seems to flash or blink every time the lighthouse lantern swings toward us, the pulsar's beam of radio energy seems to "pulse" every time it swings toward Earth. Pulsars can spin incredibly rapidly, up to hundreds of times a second. Pulsars also make a regular clicking noise as their beam swings past Earth, like the ticking of a precise clock. Dr. Wolszczan was studying those that spin at a rate of *thousands* of times a second.

He found that one pulsar—PSR 1257+12—had something odd about its pulse. Sometimes the pulse came a minute fraction of a second late, while other times it came a fraction of a second early. Theoretically, this is impossible, unless the pulsar had planets orbiting it. If planets swung around the pulsar, their gravity would pull it first toward Earth and then away. This could affect the timing of the pulses.

Wolszczan believed that there were two planets orbiting PSR 1257+12. One was about three times the mass of Earth and took about 98 days to circle the pulsar, and the other was about 3.5 times the size of Earth and orbited in just over 66 days. Both planets were roughly the same distance from the pulsar that Mercury is from the Sun. There was also the possibility of the existence of at least two other planets.

(43)

Astronomers call a number of very different objects "dwarfs." Brown dwarfs form similarly to stars but don't have enough gravity to initiate a fusion reaction. They range in size from 13 to 75 times the mass of Jupiter. White dwarfs, on the other hand, are stars, but they are very old ones that can no longer shine through atomic fusion. Without this outward energy to balance their gravity, they have collapsed into very small objects, perhaps no larger than Earth. This not only makes them very dense, but they also become white-hot from the collapse. Red dwarfs are ordinary stars, but they are smaller, cooler—and hence redder—than our own Sun. **Yellow dwarf** stars are actually among the most common of stars. They are considered average or normal stars, and our Sun is one of them.

BROWN, WHITE, RED, AND YELLOW DWARFS

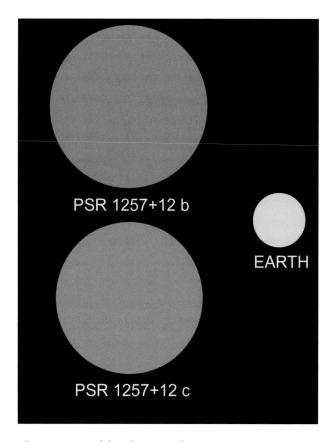

The two possible planets orbiting PSR 1257+12 are at least three times the size of Earth.

It was an exciting discovery—the first evidence of planets around a star other than the Sun. Such worlds would be terribly harsh, though, with little chance of life existing on them. Pulsars are powerful emitters of X rays, and the intense radiation would be deadly. This worried some astronomers. It was wonderful to have found these new planets, but pulsars are strange, hostile objects. What if it was only a weird fluke that planets formed around one of them? Or what if planets were more likely to form around pulsars than around stars like the Sun? So far, there were only two examples of stars having planets: the Sun and PSR 1257+12—but the pulsar is not a typical star in any way. Astronomers hoped to discover a planet around a star similar to our own Sun.

The Planet Hunters

Michel Mayor and Didier Queloz, astronomers with the Geneva Observatory in Switzerland, began searching for the telltale wobble in stars that indicates the possibility of planets. In 1995, after examining 150 stars, they found a planet orbiting the star 51 Pegasi. The planet is much bigger than Earth, but still only about half the mass of Jupiter. It is far too small to be a brown dwarf. It was discovered using the Doppler technique, which also showed that the planet orbited very close to its sun, at only about 4.3 million miles (7 million km)—so close that the new planet's "year" is only four days long. This is much closer than Mercury is to our Sun, which it orbits at about 35 million miles (57 million km).

It would be impossible for life to exist on the planet orbiting 51 Pegasi because of the intense heat of the planet's surface.

The new planet may be a very strange world indeed, and an awful one. It is so close to its sun that its surface temperature is over 1,830°F (1,000°C), hot enough to bring rock to a red heat or to melt lead, tin, or silver. Since it's very unlikely that a large planet could have formed so close to a star, it has been suggested that it formed much farther out—perhaps as much as 457 million miles (735 million km) away—and later began to approach the star as the result of tidal effects. The planet is probably nearly a molten ball of rock and iron, seven times the diameter of Earth and with seven times the surface gravity. The glowing landscape may flow slowly under its own weight, so that mountains and craters are less permanent than a hole scooped in thick mud.

It would be just as impossible for life to exist on 51 Pegasi's planet as on the planets orbiting PSR 1257+12. Still there is a fundamental difference: 51 Pegasi is a star similar to the Sun. If its only known planet orbits too close to it to permit life, there may be planets orbiting farther away. Temperatures on them might be moderate enough to permit water to exist in liquid form. Since there is at least one other sunlike star that possesses planets it is likely that there might be others.

Just over a year later, in January 1996, Geoffrey Marcy and Paul Butler discovered another extrasolar system. They announced that they had discovered planets orbiting the stars 70 Virginis and 47 Ursae Majoris. Both are stars similar to our Sun. The planet said to be orbiting 70 Virginis, a star a little cooler and older than our Sun, has a mass about nine times that of Jupiter—so it might be only a brown dwarf. This planet orbits its sun at about half the distance of Earth from the Sun. While its surface may still be

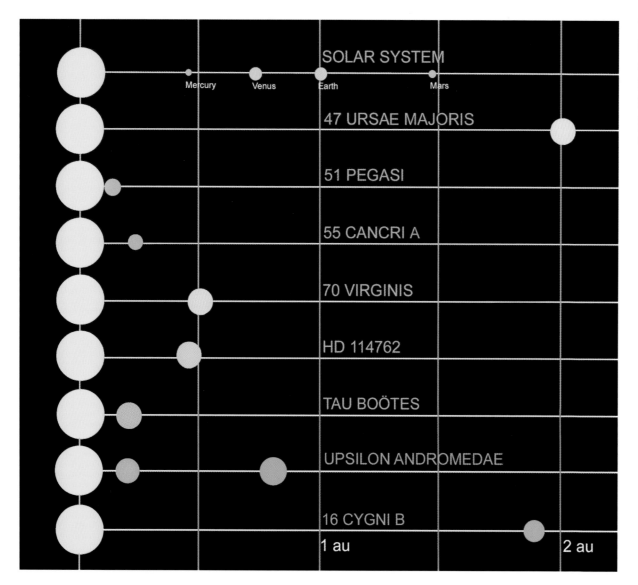

SOLAR SYSTEM

Mercury   Venus   Earth   Mars

47 URSAE MAJORIS

51 PEGASI

55 CANCRI A

70 VIRGINIS

HD 114762

TAU BOÖTES

UPSILON ANDROMEDAE

16 CYGNI B

1 au   2 au

This diagram shows the distance of some extrasolar planets to their sun as compared to the distance of the planets in our solar system to our Sun.

(47)

hot—about 185°F (85°C)—it's below the boiling point of water, so organic molecules may be able to exist there. In fact, Marcy has suggested that the planet may possess oceans and rainfall; other astronomers think that the planet may be a gas giant with no solid surface on which water could collect. So far, the evidence is too skimpy for anyone to be certain.

The potential planet orbiting 47 Ursae Majoris has a mass of only about 2.5 times that of Jupiter. It orbits its star at a distance of about twice that of Earth from the Sun, taking about three years to make one orbit. With a surface temperature of only 194°F (90°C) it, too, may be able to support liquid water.

In April 1996, Marcy and Butler announced that they found yet another extrasolar planet, a body orbiting the star Rho 1 Cancri. Its mass is about the same as Jupiter's, and it orbits at only about 0.11 AU from its sun. Like 51 Pegasi's planet, this, too, may be a very hot world, with a surface temperature of about 240°F (115°C). The two astronomers believe that they may also have some evidence of a second planet. It may be about five times the mass of Jupiter, taking about eight years to orbit Rho 1 Cancri.

Since the mid-1990s the number of extrasolar planets discovered has risen to nearly 100, and the number is continually growing.

The planet orbiting the star 51 Pegasi was the first to be discovered orbiting an average star beyond our own solar system. It is a gas giant many times larger than Jupiter. Most extrasolar planets discovered since then have been found to be similar gas giants. There are other types of planets, but the reason so many gas giants are found is simple: They're *big*. Even though modern instruments and techniques are incredibly sensitive, an Earth-sized planet is a very small object to find, especially if it is many light-years away. A small world would have such a slight effect on its star that it would be almost—but not quite—impossible to detect.

Large planets are easier to spot because the effect of their mass on their stars is proportionally greater. Even a planet considerably smaller than Jupiter, such as the one orbiting star HD46375, only one-fourth the mass of Jupiter, is still some 80 times the mass of Earth. Uranus, the smallest of the gas giants in our own solar system, is 22 times less massive than Jupiter, but it still outmasses Earth by nearly 1,400 percent. Our solar system contains both gas giants (four of them) and rocky, earthlike worlds (five of them), so it is reasonable to suppose that a star with one or more gas giants would also possess smaller, terrestrial planets if planets form the same way everywhere.

CHAPTER SIX.
NEW WORLDS

Most of the planets discovered recently have no names—at least not names in the sense that Jupiter, Mars, and Venus have names. Instead, astronomers give the planets designations based on the name of the star they orbit. A letter, starting with "b," is added to the name of the star in the order that planets are discovered. For example, the first planet discovered orbiting 51 Pegasi is called 51 Pegasi b. If two more planets are discovered, they would be called 51 Pegasi c and 51 Pegasi d. If two or more planets of another star are discovered at the same time, the one nearest the star would be called "b," the next one out "c," and so on.

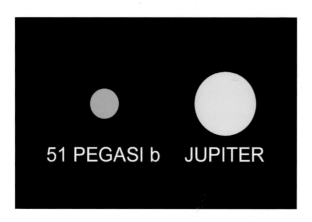

51 PEGASI b   JUPITER

51 Pegasi b

The first planet found orbiting a star like our Sun, 51 Pegasi b (which orbits the star 51 Pegasi) could hardly be less like Earth. Nearly half the size of Jupiter, it orbits 20 times closer to its sun than Earth orbits our own Sun. The face of 51 Pegasi b is probably turned permanently toward its sun. Under a sun looming 20 times larger in its sky than our Sun appears from Earth, a sun that never rises and never sets, 51 Pegasi b has a surface temperature over 2,200°F (1,200°C), hot enough to melt silver, gold, and copper. If 51 Pegasi b is a giant terrestrial planet, it would have a molten surface with an atmosphere of metallic vapor. The powerful **tidal forces** caused by the nearby star would make the planet volcanically active.

On the other hand, 51 Pegasi b may be a gas giant, like a small Jupiter. In this case, superheated gases in the atmosphere would flow in a constant stream from the hot side to the cooler dark side of the planet. In the illustration to the facing page, 51 Pegasi b is seen from a small moon as the planet eclipses its sun. 51 Pegasi may emit superflares occasionally—a pair of these enormous eruptions are shown here jetting beyond the limb, or edge, of the planet. If the heat of the sun weren't enough, the intense radiation from these flares would prevent life from existing on 51 Pegasi b.

When you look at the stars on a dark, clear night, you will notice that they are not all points of white light, but that many of them are colored. Betelgeuse, the bright star in the "shoulder" of the constellation Orion, for instance, is distinctly red. The color of a star is an indication of its temperature. The redder a star is, the cooler it is, while stars that are white or bluish are very hot—just as when a bar of iron is heated, it first glows dull red; then, as it grows hotter, it becomes brighter, glowing orange, then yellow and then white hot. Astronomers use the colors of stars to classify them in much the same way that a biologist classifies insects or flowers according to their distinctive characteristics.

In decreasing order of temperature, stars are designated O, B, A, F, G, K, and M, as shown in the diagram on the following page. O stars are hot blue-violet, while M stars are cool red. Our Sun is a yellow G-type star, which lies in the middle of the range. Each category has ten or more divisions, for even finer distinctions. For example, a G5 star and a G3 star would both be yellow, but the G5 would be a little hotter than the G3. Stars are also classified according to their size: Ia, Iab, and Ib are supergiants, II are bright giants, III are giants, IV are sub-giants, V are dwarfs, and VI are white dwarfs. Stars usually have labels like this: G3V, which is a yellow dwarf (like our Sun), or M6Ia, which is a red supergiant.

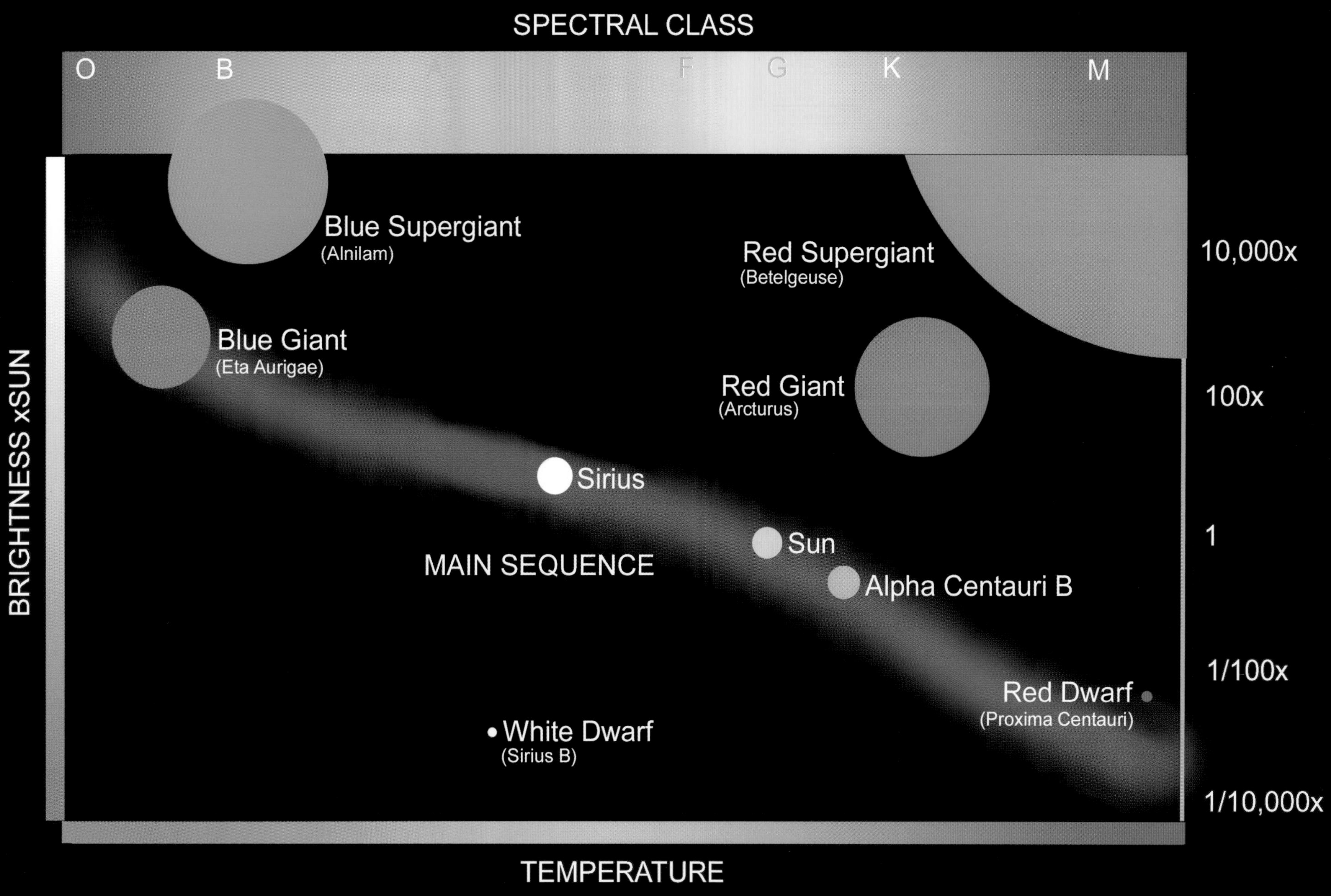

SPECTRAL CLASS

O   B   A   F   G   K   M

Blue Supergiant
(Alnilam)

Red Supergiant
(Betelgeuse)

10,000x

Blue Giant
(Eta Aurigae)

Red Giant
(Arcturus)

100x

BRIGHTNESS xSUN

Sirius

MAIN SEQUENCE

Sun

1

Alpha Centauri B

1/100x

Red Dwarf
(Proxima Centauri)

• White Dwarf
(Sirius B)

1/10,000x

TEMPERATURE

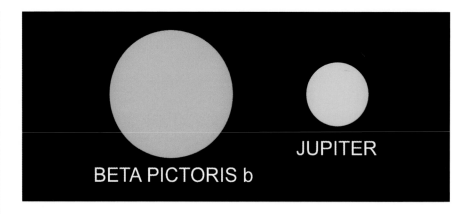

BETA PICTORIS b

JUPITER

DUST RING

PLANET

A simplified view of the dust disk surrounding Beta Pictoris shows how the planets have cleared empty spaces between the rings.

Beta Pictoris b

Beta Pictoris is a Type A5V star, larger and hotter than our own Sun. It is nearly 60 light-years from Earth. It has a flat disk of dust and gas surrounding it, but no one knows for sure if it has any planets orbiting it. This disk is about 100AU to 500AU in radius, which means that it is 100 to 500 times the size of Earth's orbit around the Sun. The discovery of a gap in the ring may indicate the possible existence of a planet within the disk. The gap is similar to the large gap called Cassini's Division in Saturn's ring. Many astronomers believe that there may be a planet—perhaps even two—within this gap, sweeping the gap clean of dust as the planet orbits Beta Pictoris. The possible planet may be at about 20AU and have a mass about five times that of Earth. In addition to the possibility of one or more planets, there is also evidence that comets orbit the star. One of Beta Pictoris's planets, Beta Pictoris b, shown on the facing page, could be a giant Jupiter-like world with a dust ring seen in the distance.

(54)

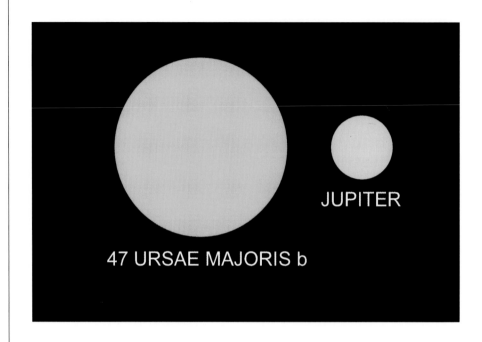

JUPITER

47 URSAE MAJORIS b

47 Ursae Majoris b

47 Ursae Majoris b is 2.8 times the size of Jupiter. It orbits a little more than twice the distance of Earth from the Sun, so it is a cold world. It is large enough to have moons the size of Mars orbiting it. 47 Ursae Majoris b is shown on the facing page from one of its possible moons. Even though the moon has an earthlike atmosphere, its rocky surface is covered with a thick mantle of ice.

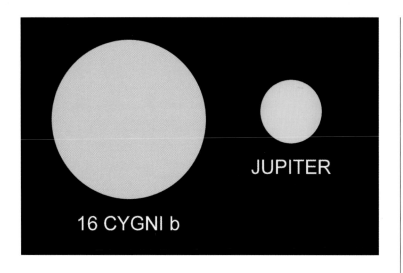

16 CYGNI b

JUPITER

16 Cygni B b

16 Cygni B is part of a **binary star** system. Binary stars orbit around each other like two ice-skaters holding hands. They are so common—more than half the stars in our galaxies are pairs—that lone stars like our Sun are the exception rather than the rule. Binary stars come in all sorts of combinations: The two stars may be nearly identical, or they can be quite different, as in a red giant and white dwarf pair. The other star in the 16 Cygni binary is called 16 Cygni A. The two are about 1,100AU apart.

16 Cygni B b, the planet orbiting 16 Cygni B, a star very much like our own, was discovered in 1996. It is about five times as massive as Jupiter (that is, it is as heavy as five planets the size of Jupiter). It is thought to be a small brown dwarf, orbiting about 1.8AU from its sun every 800 days. Its orbit may once have been more circular, but tidal forces caused by 16 Cygni A have distended it into an extreme ellipse. This takes it as close to its star as Venus's distance from the Sun and then as far away as Mars's distance. Great temperature changes may cause drastic climactic changes to the planet. On the facing page, 16 Cygni B b is seen in the sky from a large, earthlike moon.

16 Cygni B b is shown here from the surface of one of its moons. The planet is at its farthest distance from its sun, 16 Cygni B, and all of the water vapor in the moon's atmosphere has frozen onto its own frigid surface.

This scene from one of its moons shows 16 Cygni b at its closest distance to its sun, which now looms twice as large as before in the sky. All the ice and snow has evaporated, filling the moon's atmosphere with a foggy mist.

Lalande 21185 b

Lalande 21185, a red dwarf, is another star that may or may not have a planet. If it does, the planet may be between 0.5 to 2 times the mass of Jupiter, orbiting about 9.5AU from the star—nearly ten times farther than Earth is from the Sun. George Gatewood, an astronomer, announced the possibility of this planet, and suggested that there might actually be two planets, the second one less massive than Jupiter and about 3.5AU from Lalande 21185. The planet is shown above from one of its moons as a cold, dark world far from its dim red sun.

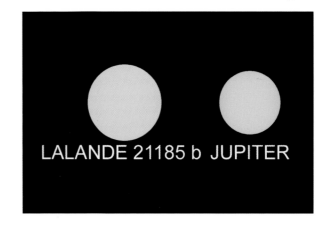

LALANDE 21185 b JUPITER

Proxima Centauri eclipsed
by a moon

Proxima Centauri b

Proxima Centauri is the star closest to our own Sun—only 4.3 light-years away. It is a red dwarf that may have a very large planet orbiting it at about the distance of Venus from the Sun. On the facing page we see Proxima Centauri, which is a violent flare star, as one of the planet's moons eclipses it.

55 Cancri A b & c

55 Cancri A is a binary star with a distant red dwarf companion. One planet orbits this sunlike star, and it is possible that there is at least one more. The known planet is a Jupiter-size world orbiting approximately every fifteen days at a distance of only .11 AU—one-tenth the distance of Earth from the Sun. The second possible planet, 55 Cancri A c, would orbit at the distance of Saturn from the Sun. On the following spread we see this planet—which is about five times the size of Jupiter—from a large icy moon.

55 Cancri A c .

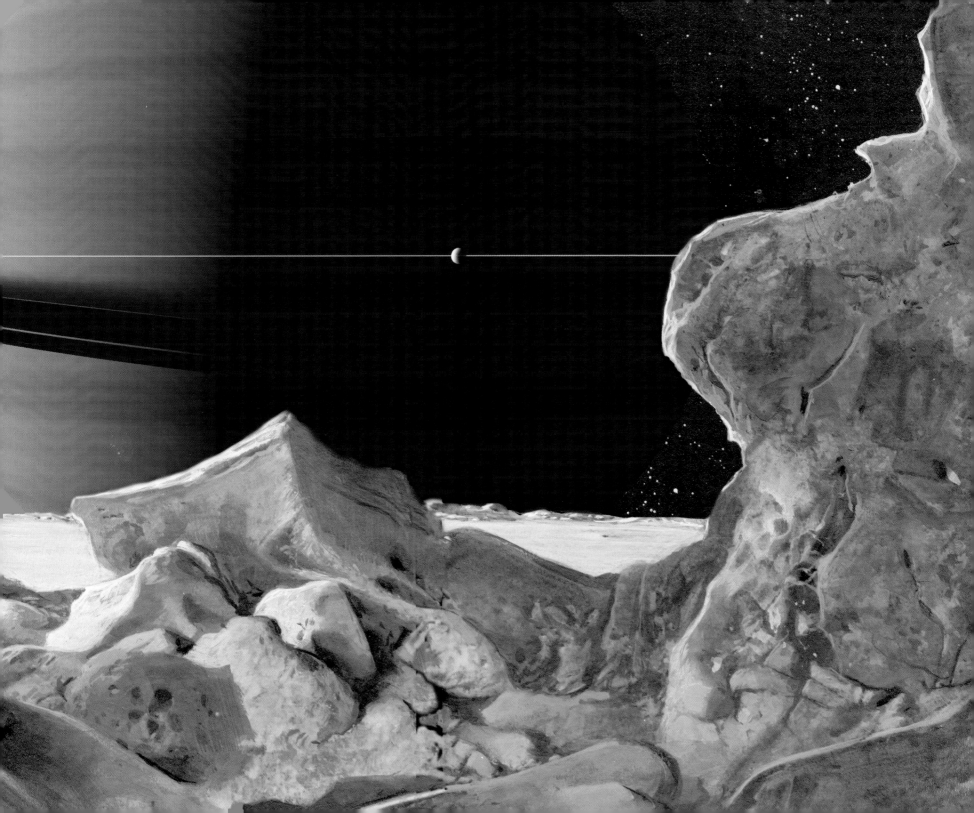

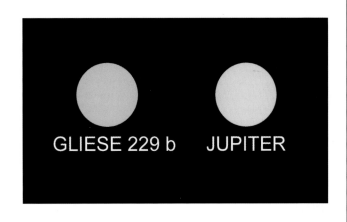

GLIESE 229 b   JUPITER

Gliese 229 b

The planet orbiting Gliese 229 is probably too large to be a true planet; it may instead be a brown dwarf. It is so large that it is heated to a dim red glow by its own gravity, but it is not quite large enough to trigger the fusion reaction that would transform it into a full-fledged star. Although Gliese 229 b is 40 times the mass of Jupiter, it is compressed into a size not much larger than Jupiter. The planet orbits more than 40 times farther from its star than Earth is from the Sun, and any moons it may have would receive more heat from the planet than from its distant star. On the facing page we see Gliese 229 b from one of these moons. Although the night side of the planet looms above the horizon, it glows red-hot from its internal heat. The moon, affected by the powerful tidal forces and heated by the incandescent planet, is volcanically active.

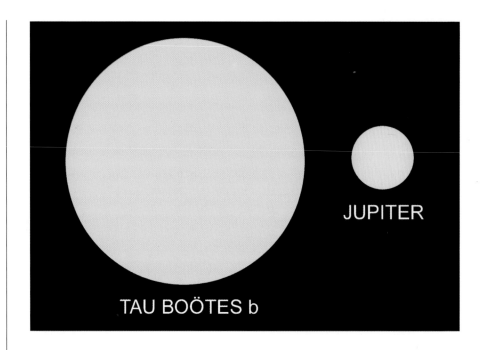

JUPITER

TAU BOÖTES b

Tau Boötes b

Tau Boötes is a star similar to the Sun, though very much hotter and brighter. It may have a planet 3.8 times the mass of Jupiter orbiting only 0.046AU away—eight times closer than Mercury is to the Sun. This would cause it to have a surface temperature of 1,240°F (671°C), and it would orbit Tau Boötes in only 3.3 days. The planet, while four times more massive than Jupiter, may be only slightly larger. It is so close to its intensely hot star that the planet may be slowly evaporating, its atmosphere streaming away into space like the tail of a comet.

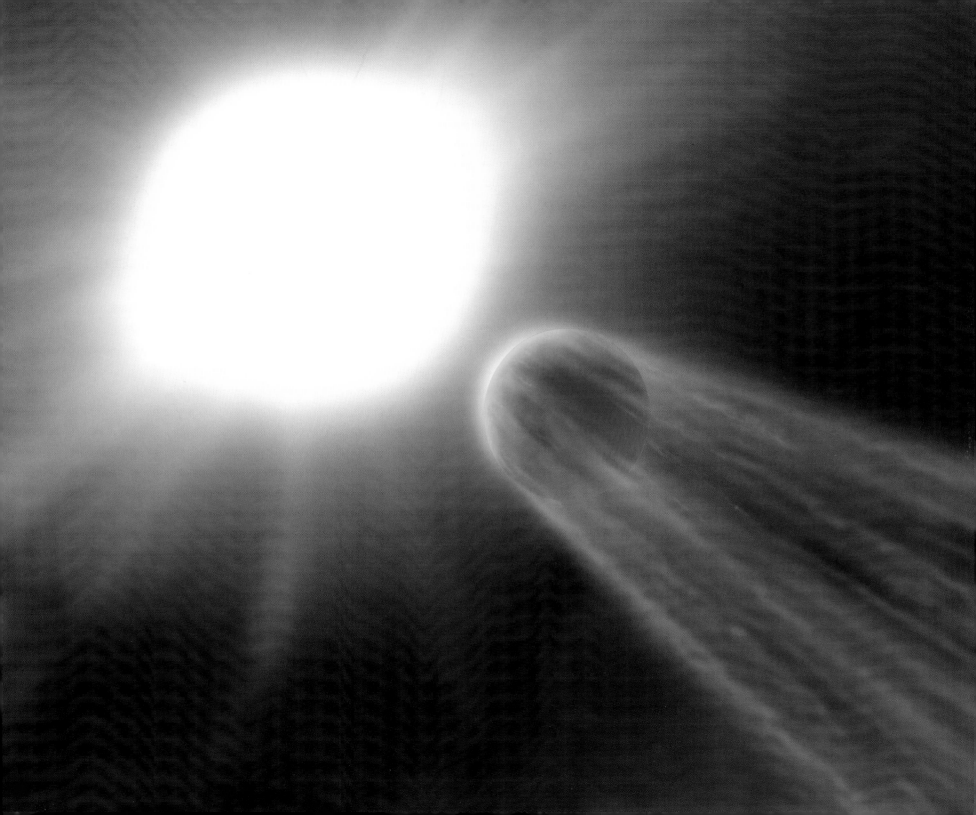

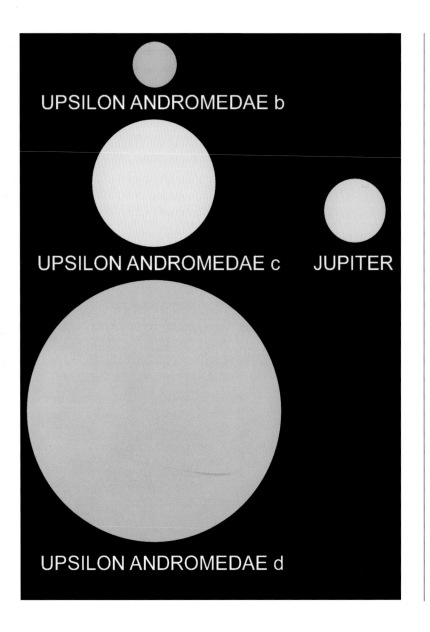

UPSILON ANDROMEDAE b

UPSILON ANDROMEDAE c   JUPITER

UPSILON ANDROMEDAE d

Upsilon Andromedae b, c, and d

Upsilon Andromedae, a star very similar to the Sun, may have three planets, designated b, c, and d. This is the first multi-planet system to be discovered. The planet nearest the star, b, is a little more than half the mass of Jupiter and orbits at a distance of 0.057AU, taking about four and a half days. It has a diameter about 1.2 times that of Jupiter. Because it is so close to its star, it has a surface temperature of about 3,000°F (1,650°C)—hot enough to melt nickel and iron. The planet probably keeps one side permanently facing its sun. This causes the atmosphere to become superheated—so much that it might actually ignite. Flaming hot gases rush away from the intensely hot subsolar point, flowing in all directions toward the cooler night side, as shown in the illustration on the following page.

Upsilon Andromedae c is 1.98 times the mass of Jupiter and orbits at about 0.83AU—about the same distance Venus is from the Sun. It is not an incandescent inferno like the inner planet, but it is still probably too hot for life. Hot atmospheric gases form a high mist above the permanent cloud cover, causing the planet to appear bluish. It is large enough to have very large moons. It is shown on pages 72-73 from a moon the size of Mars.

The most distant planet, Upsilon Andromedae d, is more than four times as massive as Jupiter and is more than 2.5 times as far from its star as Earth is from the Sun, taking about 3.5 to 4 years to make one orbit. The planet, so far from its star, may be a cold, Jupiter-like world big enough to have moons the size of Mars or even larger. We see it on pages 74-75 from one of these giant moons, accompanied by many of its other moons, including one with an atmosphere like Earth's.

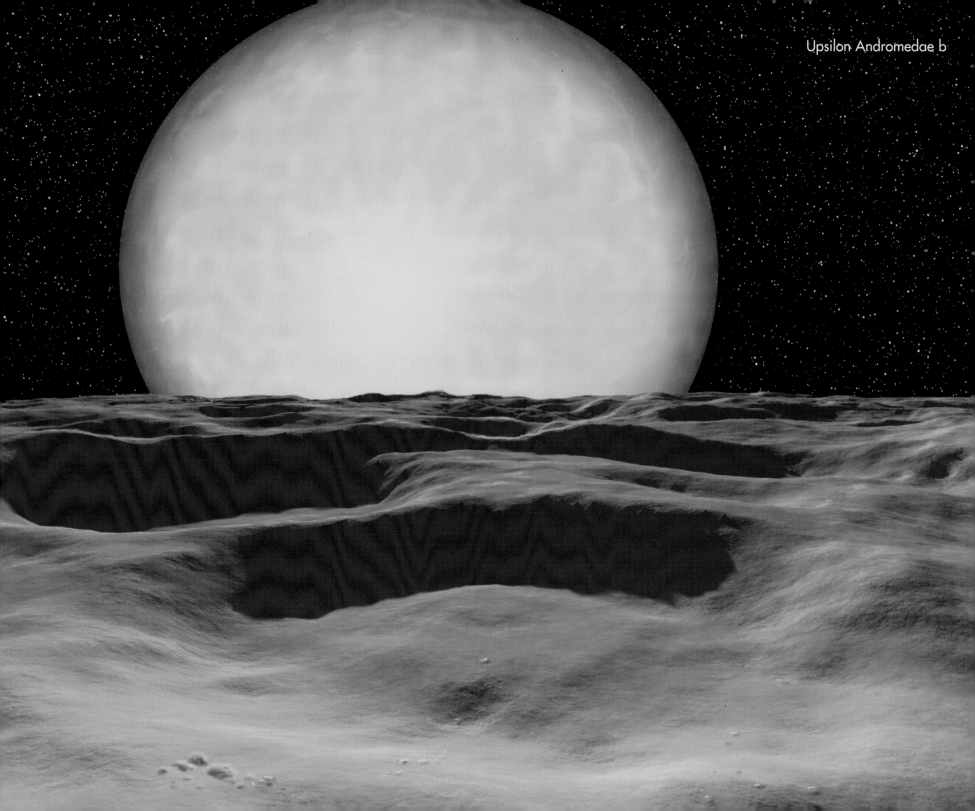

Upsilon Andromedae c
(to the right) as seen
from one of its moons

Upsilon Andromedae d
(to the right) seen from
one of its giant moons

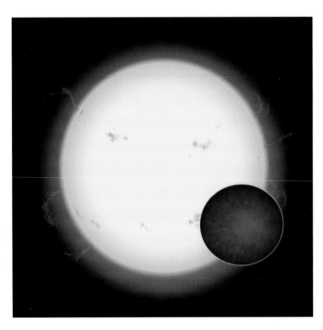

Here we see the giant planet HD 209458 b as it passes in front of its star, only 0.045 AU away—more than 20 times closer than Earth is to our Sun.

HD 209458 b

The planet-hunting team of Geoffrey Marcy and Paul Butler discovered in 1999 that a sunlike K1 star named HD 209548 possesses a planet. The planet, HD 209458 b, is about 0.7 times as massive as Jupiter and orbits about 0.045AU from its star. Thus its surface temperature is about 2,070°F (1,132°C), hot enough to melt copper, gold, tin, and silver. The astronomers predicted that the planet might pass between its sun and Earth, and that this event might be detectable. Astronomer Greg Henry was able to observe a 1.7 percent drop in HD 209458's brightness as the planet passed in front of it. This was the first time that a distant planet had been seen passing in front of its star. It helped confirm the existence of the planet, which until that time had only been deduced from the Doppler shifts of the star. The amount of the star's dimming also provided much valuable information about the size and density of the new planet. As Henry said, "We've essentially seen the shadow of the planet and used it to measure the planet's size."

The planet is 0.69 percent as massive as Jupiter, but it is 60 percent larger. This means that it is a ball of gas, like Jupiter. Since gas giant planets cannot form so close to a star, it must have formed much farther away and gradually migrated closer, probably as gravitational effects degraded its orbit. In the illustration on the facing page, HD 209458 b is seen from a nearby asteroid. The giant planet's red-hot atmosphere is streaming from the sunlit side to the cooler dark side. The star, HD 209458, which is more than 20 times closer than our Sun to Earth, is about to appear from behind the planet.

A brown dwarf and its dust rings are seen here from a nearby asteroid.

Brown Dwarf

One of the most recent discoveries in the search for extrasolar planets is that rings of dust surround many brown dwarf stars. This suggests that brown dwarfs may have formed like normal stars and therefore may have planets of their own. A planet orbiting a brown dwarf would be a very cold, dim, inhospitable place since these stars radiate very little heat and light.

Aldeberan b

The star that Aldeberan b orbits is unlike most of the other stars we have found planets circling. Aldeberan is a red giant 115 times larger than our Sun and 90 times brighter. The planet that orbits it is 11 times larger than Jupiter—more than 120 times larger than Earth. Like Jupiter, Aldeberan b is a gas giant. This planet orbits close to the huge star, only slightly farther than Earth orbits from our much smaller Sun, so Aldeberan looms in the sky like an enormous red balloon, which is illustrated on pages 80-81.

Aldeberan is a red giant star
115 times larger than our Sun.

PSR 1257+12 b, c, and d

The planets that orbit pulsars such as PSR 1257+12 may be the strangest planets known. A pulsar is all that remains of a dying star, one that has blown away most of its mass in a violent explosion called a **supernova**. The rapidly spinning core of the star is all that remains, an incredibly massive object smaller than Earth. The planets orbiting PSR 1257+12 may be all that is left of the Jupiter-like planets that once orbited the star. When the star exploded, it stripped away the planets' atmospheres, leaving little more behind than their bare, rocky cores. The tiny pulsar shown on the facing page is seen from one of these distant, frigid, utterly dead worlds.

Planets Without Suns

The strangest of all the new planets discovered are also the most mysterious. They don't fit the traditional definition of "planet," since they have no central star around which they orbit. Instead, they drift in the starless void of empty space. Eighteen of these strange worlds have been found in the Sigma Orionis star cluster, which is in the constellation Orion. These must be bleak, cold, dark worlds with no sun to light or warm them. Their only illumination is the faint light of the stars in a sky that is perpetually night. These planets seem to be large—from 5 to 13 times more massive than Jupiter—though they are too small to be brown dwarfs. They appear to be planetlike in size and composition, but no one has been able to explain how they were able to form without a star.

A pulsar is seen in the distance from a bare, rocky planet.

Future Worlds?

More and more planets beyond our solar system are being discovered all the time, but all of them are giant and supergiant planets—or even brown dwarfs—that resemble Jupiter much more than they resemble Earth. Astronomers can only speculate that small planets might also exist. But the chances of finding planets like our own are rather slim. Current telescopes are just not powerful enough. Planets like Earth are hundreds and even thousands of times smaller than the giant worlds we have discovered. The effects of the gravitational pull on their stars would be nearly impossible to detect. And since planets give off no light of their own, seeing one would be extraordinarily difficult.

But it is not impossible. Incredibly powerful telescopes are being built right now and even more powerful ones are planned. Soon, the Hubble Space Telescope will be replaced by a larger, more powerful instrument—one that might be capable of detecting the faint traces of earthlike worlds. But even if we found such worlds, we might never be able to determine whether or not they bear life . . . at least not in the foreseeable future. Of course, the hope remains that there might be life on them. It is this drive to find our neighbors in space that keeps the search for extrasolar planets alive.

In 2000, scientists were surprised to discover eighteen planets wandering free, unattached to any star. These Jupiter-like gas giants are dark, cold places with no sun to light or warm them. In the background of this rogue planet is the Horsehead Nebula—a black cloud shaped like a horse's head that is part of a star cluster in the constellation Orion, where these planets were first found.

accretion: a process in which small particles of dust and gas stick together to form larger particles.

asteroids: chunks of rock and metal debris left over from the creation of the solar system.

astrometry: the study of the position and movement of the stars; from Latin words meaning "star measuring."

astronomical unit (AU): the average distance of Earth from the Sun, which is approximately 93 million miles (150 million km).

binary star: a pair of stars that orbit each other.

blink comparator: an instrument an astronomer uses to compare photographs of the stars taken on different nights in order to determine if any changes have occurred.

brown dwarf: a large planetlike body too small for nuclear fusion to start, which would make it a true star, but large enough to glow from the heat produced by its own gravity.

comet: an icy interplanetary body that releases gases that form a bright head and long tail when heated by the Sun.

density: the proportion of mass to volume. The more mass there is in any particular volume, the denser it is. A container of water is denser than a same size container of air because its molecules are packed closer together.

Doppler effect: a shift in the wavelength of light or sound as perceived by the observer of an approaching or receding object. The speed of a moving object can be determined by this shift. (Named after the Austrian scientist Christian Doppler, who was the first to describe the effect.)

eclipsing binary: a binary star system in which the stars eclipse each other during each revolution when seen from Earth.

extrasolar: outside our solar system.

fusion: the process by which two atomic nuclei are combined to make a new atom, thereby releasing energy.

Galilean satellites: the four largest moons of the planet Jupiter; named for their discoverer, Galileo Galilei.

gas giant: a large planet composed mostly of gas and liquid, usually with only a small, rocky core.

gravitational contraction: the slow contraction, or shrinking, of a cloud of dust, a planet, or a star due to its gravity. Heat and radiation are created in the process.

gravity: the force by which all masses attract all other masses.

mass: the amount of material in an object. For example, Jupiter is much more massive than Earth because it contains more material, but it is also less dense than Earth because this material is spread though a greater volume.

moon: 1. (cap.) Earth's natural satellite. 2. any satellite orbiting a planet.

Oort Cloud: the swarm of comets that orbits our solar system beyond the orbit of Pluto.

planet: any solid or partially liquid body that orbits a star but is too small to generate energy by nuclear reactions.

planetesimal: one of the small bodies from which planets form.

protoplanetary disk: the disk of dust and gas surrounding a star that eventually accretes into planetesimals and then into planets.

protostar: a cloud of dust and gas that contracts into a star.

pulsar: a rapidly rotating neutron star that emits strong pulses of radiation.

red dwarf: a small, cool star that

only radiates a modest amount of heat.

solar system: a sun and all of the bodies that orbit it.

spectrograph: an instrument that creates and records an image of a spectrum.

spectrum: the rainbow of colors that forms when light is passed through a prism.

star: a body usually made entirely of gas that is massive enough to have initiated nuclear reactions in its core.

supernova: a very powerful exploding star. In the explosion, most of the star's mass is blown away, leaving only its very dense core behind.

terrestrial planet: a planet with a rocky surface similar to Earth.

tidal forces: The effect of an uneven pull of gravity, which does not act equally over an object. The part of an object that is farthest from a planet is pulled on less than the side that is closest to the planet. This unequal pull can cause stresses which, if strong enough, can cause volcanic eruptions or even tear the smaller body apart.

yellow dwarf: among the most common of stars. They are considered average or normal, and our Sun is one of them.

white dwarf: a planet-sized star of about the same mass as our Sun. It is one of the end states of a dying star.

Web sites

Extrasolar Planets
http://www.exoplanets.org

Extrasolar Planets Catalog
http//www.astronautica.com

Extrasolar Planets Encyclopedia
http://www.obspm.fr/encycl/
encycl.html

Extrasolar Visions
http://www.jtwinc.com/
extrasolar/

Galileo
Official National Aeronautics
and Space Administration/Jet
Propulsion Laboratory
(NASA/JPL) site devoted to the
Galileo space probe.
http://galileo/jpl.nasa.gov

Live from the Sun
An excellent source of information about the Sun, with links to
many related Web sites.
http://www.fsus.fsu.edu/
mcquone/InvestUniv/LvfromSn.
htm

NASA Spacelink
Gateway to many NASA Web
sites about the Sun and planets.
http://spacelink.msfc.nasa.gov/
index.html

Nine Planets
Detailed information about the
Sun, the planets, and all the
moons, along with many photos
and useful links to other Web
sites.
http://www.nineplanets.org

Planet Orbits
A free software program that allows the user to see the positions of all the planets in the solar system at one time.
http://www.alcyone.de

Planet's Visibility
A free software program that allows users to find out when they can see any particular planet and where in the sky to look for it.
http://www.alcyone.de

Solar System Simulator
An amazing Web site that allows visitors to travel to all the planets and their moons and to create their own views of these distant worlds.
http://space.jpl.nasa.gov/

Books

Beatty, J. Kelly, Carolyn Collins Petersen and Andrew Chaikin, eds. *The New Solar System.* Cambridge, MA: Sky Publishing, 1999.

Clay, Rebecca. *Stars and Galaxies.* Brookfield, CT: Twenty-First Century Books, 1997.

Fradin, Dennis Brindell. *The Planet Hunters.* New York: Margaret K. McElderry Books, 1997.

Hartmann, William K. *Moons and Planets.* Belmont, CA: Wadsworth Publishing Co., 1999.

Hartmann, William K., and Ron Miller. *The History of Earth.* New York: Workman Publishing Co., 1992.

Miller, Ron, and William K. Hartmann. *The Grand Tour.* New York: Workman Publishing Co., 1993.

Scagell, Robine. *The New Book of Space.* Brookfield, CT: Copper Beech, 1997.

Schaaf, Fred. *Planetology.* Danbury, CT: Franklin Watts, 1996.

Vogt, Gregory L. *Deep Space Astronomy.* Brookfield, CT: Twenty-First Century Books, 1999.

Magazines

Astronomy
www.astronomy.com/

Sky & Telescope
www.skypub.com

Organizations

American Astronomical Society
2000 Florida Avenue NW, Suite
400
Washington, DC 20009-1231
http://www.AAS.org

Association of Lunar and
 Planetary Observers
P.O. Box 171302
Memphis, TN 38187-1302
http://www.lpl.arizona.edu/alpo/

Astronomical Society of
 the Pacific
390 Ashton Avenue
San Francisco, CA 94112
http://www.aspsky.org

The Planetary Society
65 N. Catalina Avenue
Pasadena, CA 91106
http://planetary.org

Ron Miller is an illustrator and writer who specializes in scientific subjects. His special interest has always been astronomy and he has created or contributed to many books on this subject, including *Cycles of Fire, The History of Earth,* and *The Grand Tour.* Among his nonfiction books for young people are *The History of Rockets* and *The History of Science Fiction.* Miller has designed a set of ten commemorative stamps on the planets in our solar system for the U.S. Postal Service. He has written several novels and has worked on a number of science fiction films, such as *Dune* and *Total Recall.* His work has won many awards and distinctions, and his original paintings can be found in collections all over the world, including that of the National Air and Space Museum in Washington, D.C., and magazines such as *National Geographic, Scientific American, Sky and Telescope,* and *Natural History.* Miller lives in Fredericksburg, Virginia, with his wife and five cats.